What My Daddy Should Have Told Me

Life Lessons for the African-American Male

Rickie Clark

ISBN: 978-1518779046
ISBN-13: 1518779042

Foreword

Dear Reader,

This book is a compilation of short essays about "Things I Wish My Daddy Would Have Told Me." It consists of some special life events compiled to give hope and help to African American males. It can also be used as a tool for those who mentor youth. Especially for those mentors who are more than troubled about the future of young Men of Color. This book is not scientifically oriented. It has not been tried and tested by any great studies and I have not completed any educational research. It isn't based on the theories of Freud, Piaget, Skinner or other similar experts. I couldn't wait for that. Nor could I wait for just the right words to be placed properly and in the right order or be overly concerned about the political correctness of all the content. I could not wait to tell my story about my journey to manhood. I feel that we must begin to work diligently and immediately to try to save our young men. We must never forget that if they are destroyed as a boy, they will never become a man.

This book was written to meet a need.... To do something, or say something, or at least something more.... "Until better information can be written." Our young men are dying daily in every city, homeland and rural place. We read and hear about many, but a large percentage are killed violently and we don't ever hear their story.

There are a lot of young men who suffer in silence. They never get the opportunity to speak up about the injustices and the violations that they suffer. Then there are those who look at what is going on around them and believe these acts are merely a way of life.

Today there are many young men who are unable to escape the evil and painful grip of not having a Daddy in their life. They have missed out on some of the valuable lessons that a father can teach his son. There was no Daddy around to teach them about SPIRITUALITY, EDUCATION, HIS-STORY, CHILD SUPPORT, WHAT TO DO WHEN STOPPED BY THE POLICE, MONEY or MANHOOD.

Hopefully this book can guide them in the right direction. I pray that something is said that can turn someone's life around.

"IN ORDER TO BE A MAN, YOU MUST SEE A MAN"

Introduction

I've always wanted to talk to young men about Things My Daddy Should Have Told Me. Growing up on the Southeast side of Chicago, Illinois and raised by a single parent, I didn't have a lot of positive resources or role models to lead or advise me directly, or just give me information pertaining to what a man truly is.

I often wondered what kind of man I would have become if my daddy would have conversed with me pertaining to SPIRITUALITY, EDUCATION, MY HISTORY, CHILD SUPPORT, MONEY, BEING STOPPED BY THE POLICE, or MANHOOD? I have often been quoted as saying "In order to be a man you must see a man."

When I actually had the opportunity to see a man that made me realize that I too wanted to become a man. Just being in the presence of productive, conscientious minded men has ultimately changed my life entirely.

My life changing transition took place while I was employed with the Fort Worth Housing Authority's Neighbors Against Drug Program. This job was located within the Butler housing projects in Fort Worth, Texas. One of my duties was to attend a drug prevention conference hosted by African Americans in Atlanta, Georgia.

The conference speakers were predominately African-American men, such as Dr. Na'im Akbar, Dr. Wade Nobles, and Dr. Leonard Jeffries along with several other outstanding speakers.

It was at this particular conference that I learned about the Rites of Passage Programs (manhood programs). Furthermore, it was at this conference where I became conscious of the fact that not only was I not informed by my daddy about critical, real life topics, but many other African-American males were not informed as well.

After that particular conference, I instantaneously began to read a variety of books, listen to videos of speeches and lectures, and simply study topics pertaining to manhood. In fact, I feverishly attempted to assay every curriculum that I could find pertaining to being a man, as well as teaching boys to become men.

I would like to assure you that the information that I will share with you in this book did not develop in a "vacuum in the closet" or away from the real world. My intentions for writing this book are to inspire you with my life learned lessons of topics I wish my daddy would have told me. I have also been quoted as saying "You can't lead where you don't go and you can't teach what you don't know."

My abundant and unique experiences include but are not limited to raising and providing for five boys as a single parent, whereas only two were my biological sons. Moreover, I was employed with the Dallas Juvenile Detention Center, Fort Worth Housing Authority, and the Green Oaks and Charter Psychiatric Hospitals where I worked in Adolescent Chemical Dependency. Additionally, I owned and operated a community-based alternative middle and high school contractually with the Everman Independent School District for nineteen years. This nineteen year span included my duties to design, implement, and coordinate various programs pertaining to helping at risk youth. In closing, I pray to God that our boys grow up to be conscious-minded, productive, God fearing men.

Acknowledgements

Let me begin as I always do and that is by giving honor to God. I thank God for giving me the mother of all mothers Winnie Clark, the love of my life, my dad Manuel McNeal, my big brother Odell "Flip" Davis and my sisters, Vickie and Carolyn for always having my back. I give thanks to my daughter, Brittni, my sons Lil Rikki, Ashley aka "Thirsty", Mike G, Keno and David and to my Ancestors. You are like the stars in the sky, I might not see you but I know you are there.

I would like to also acknowledge my other family, the Branch's, Mr. James Branch, Sr, Dr. Elizabeth Branch and James "Scooter" Branch, Jr for trusting and believing in me when no one else did.

I must also give thanks to a host of friends and co-workers who have offered me words of encouragement, opinions, advice and contributions of relevant material.

Latisha, Tamika, Tysona, Shanavia, Marchelle "Diamond", Sherry, Mack, April, Norma, Mia, David, Donna, Karyn, Dwayne, Demetrius, Q, Ken, Mekia, Uncle Mike, Auntie Sheila, Uncle Charles, Derrick, Craig, Cathy "Pepsi", Qiana, David, Deborah, James, George, Wanda, Jeff, Pam, Byron, Charles "Mo", Cheryl, Danny, Valerie, Mike, Saturn, T. Jones, Burt, Joan, Fred, Beth, Cedric, Nikki, Alex, JaCinto, Anita, Mark, Danny, Sammie, William, Linda, Little Will, Big Cuzz, Fred, Sharon, Jan, Brian, Jasmin, Reggie, Chuck, Chris, Pedro, Kelly, Gary, Christie, YAP, Jeff, Kim, Sam G, Sonny, Q Phillip, Aunt Wezee, Chester, Vivien, Sylvia, Calvin, David, Bernard, Marsha, Al, Derek, Sheila, Kevin, Marcus, James, Bethany, Minister Lee, LaSunya, Clyde, Ben, Tony, Toyka, Big Mike, Laurene, Mrs. Wright, Ivan, Jackie, Lauren, Julia, Kofi, Donnell, Kory, Gladys, Timmy, Billy, Theresa, Mr. & Mrs. Sneed, T. Sneed, Marilyn, Jamar, Christopher Bishop R. Jordan, Darren, Jeff, Sam, Robert, Sunshyne, Michon, Jonathan, Johnny, Mary, Regina, Jaquita, T. Mann, Rita, Thea, Felicia, Daniel, Samson, Bishop Dr. Kirkla, Mrs. Birdo, Ross, Roy, Andre, Ken, Jack, Roy Brooks, Roderick, Paula, Paul, Jack, Najiba, Curtis, Donna, Donya, Mama Craddock, Larry & Reggie Kemp, Charles, Crushon, Anthony, the Zerox Twins, Derrick, Dr. S. Hill, Pan African Connection, A. J., Simon, Felix, Vincent, Darryl, Michelle, CL, Irungu, Caerese, Noni, Haggadiah, Mr. Taylor, Selena, Raymond, Kim, Tia, Dedra, Dianne, Jasper, Cynthia, Precious, Audrey, Lisa, Vanessa, Mike S, John, Cherita, Curtis, Sammy, Windy, Rev. Milton Pace, Shirley, Pharaoh, Melanie, Steve, Stacy, Rev. James Brown, Tony Johnson, Mahari.

CONTENTS

CHAPTER 1
WHAT MY DADDY SHOULD HAVE TOLD ME ABOUT SPIRITUALITY

The definition of SPIRITUALITY to me is "That which includes a sense of connection to something bigger than ourselves, and it typically involves a search for meaning in life." As such, it is a universal human experience that should impinge exceedingly on us all.

I grew up on the South Side of Chicago, Illinois. Notwithstanding, I personally never remembered any images, representation, or examples of spiritual men in my life. Additionally, my brother, uncles, friends, cousins, friends' fathers, and even my grandfather never conversed or expressed interest pertaining to SPIRITUALITY. I had to endure the absence of a father in my life and I was raised by a single mother (Winnie). Hence, it wasn't until 1979 when I enrolled into college where I started to understand SPIRITUALITY.

Even when I moved in with my grandparents, my Momma (the name I called my grandmother) would consistently make us attend church every Sunday. On the other hand, my grandfather did not attend church with us or go by himself for that matter. I felt like this was more of a religious tradition than a spiritual one. Yet, when I finally met my biological father at the age of seventeen, I was astonished to learn that he didn't go to church either. The message I perceived as a young man was that "I didn't need a spiritual relationship with the creator."

At the age of twelve, I told my grandmother that I no longer wanted to go to church and she was okay with my decision. She continued to go every Sunday, but she no longer bothered me about attending.

Hence, from what I can remember, from the age of twelve to nineteen, I was literally "unchurched." Simply put, no one ever told me that I needed to have a relationship with God or that Jesus was my Lord and Savior.

Even more alarming, I don't think any of the aforementioned men new this either. In the same manner, the few amount of boyfriends that my mother had never conversed or expressed interest pertaining to church as well. As I refer back to my youth, I do remember my friend's dads, Mr. Sneed and Mr. Franklin going to church.

My daddy should have told me about SPIRITUALITY, however, when I enrolled into Jarvis Christian College my attitude began to change. It began when I walked into the cafeteria to eat a meal. As I prepared to eat, I immediately noticed that every student I was surrounded by began to bow their heads to bless their food.

At that point I was enamored with continuously giving praise and thanking something much bigger than I could have imagined. It was then where I began to realize that God became real for me! This sensation was much bigger than my daddy, granddaddy, uncles and big brothers.

While enrolled at Jarvis Christian College, students had to take the required prerequisite religion courses. I can still remember going back to my dorm room after class, getting on my knees, and praying for about an hour. I can still remember the instructor stating "with prayer, it's like talking to God as if he was right there with you." Lord knows that at that particular time in my life, I needed to talk with God as much as possible!

As it relates to SPIRITUALITY, one of my most eye-opening experiences was being at Jarvis and being able to meet friends. More importantly, the majority of my friends' parents were preachers and preacher's wives. Also, some of my friends had uncles and grandfathers that were either pastors or associate pastors. Subsequently, it seemed as though everybody on the campus owned a Bible, except me. In fact, we had to pray before any campus approved event that we participated in.

I found that to be strange but welcomed it also. It showed me that we have to put God first before we do anything. It was at Jarvis Christian College where I truly understood what it meant to have a spiritual relationship with God.

On the contrary, Jarvis was just like other colleges and universities where students could get into just about anything, however, what stood out the most to me was that the majority of students always had a spiritual base and belief to go back to when needed. The base and belief was their relationship with God and the assuring spiritual attitude and character that would get them "back on the right track."

Jarvis Christian College was where I developed my relationship with God. Equally important, I was able to nurture my spirituality in college, and I began to thirst for a greater understanding of what SPIRITUALITY was all about. It wasn't just about religion but SPIRITUALITY, that oneness with God.

College was where I first heard God and God heard me! I remember the experiences I would have leaving Texas, and returning to Chicago. During those trips I must admit that I wouldn't take God with me, but I would always conjured up a thirst to get back to Jarvis and yearned for God.

It was in college where I became aware of what it meant to be in the presence of God and often times not knowing that God was always in my presence. I know what it means as the Bible states, "He that is in me is greater than he that is in the world."

The good thing about having a relationship with God is that once you have a personal relationship, you never want to go back. For example, it's one thing when you have an experience with God in public, however, it's a whole other thing when you have one in private.

So as I reflect on my past and my relationship with God, I wish my daddy would have told me about how much strength you will have when you "let go and let God."

Therefore, to all of the readers of this book, please humbly attempt to commit yourself wherever you are, and establish a personal relationship with a higher power. Some call him Jah, some call him Ra, some call him Jehovah, some call him Jehovah Jireh, some say the Creator and some say Allah, but I just simply call him God.

What My Daddy Should Have Told Me About Spirituality

- Spirituality is not a religion, being spiritual just means you are in touch with your own divine self (*unknown*)

- "When God has selected you, it doesn't matter who else has rejected or neglected you. God's favor outweighs all opposition." *(unknown)*

- "The phrase "Do Not Be Afraid" is written in the Bible 365 times. That's a daily reminder from God to live every day fearless. ~Godfruits.com

- "No woman wants to be in submission to a man who isn't in submission to God!" ~T.D. Jakes

- Nothing ever goes away until it has taught us what we need to know. (*unknown*)

- "The key to success is to keep growing in all areas of life – mental, emotional, spiritual, as well as physical." ~Julius Erving

- "We are not human beings having a spiritual experience. We are spiritual beings having a human experience." ~Pierre Teilhard de Chardin

CHAPTER 2

WHAT MY DADDY SHOULD HAVE TOLD ME ABOUT EDUCATION

"Education is the passport to the future for tomorrow belongs to the people who prepared for it today." ~Malcolm X

I feel like my daddy should have told me the importance of having an EDUCATION. My granddaddy was the first person to take and enroll me into public school. I can remember it as though it was yesterday.

I can still visualize my grandfather wearing black pants, a white shirt and suspenders. However, from that point on, there wasn't another male involved in my EDUCATION. This included middle and high school, and even college. In fact, there was never a male adult that conversed with me pertaining to EDUCATION.

I can even remember not having assistance with my homework or even receiving encouragement to study or read a book by a male. My daddy should have told me that EDUCATION is more than reading, is more than writing, and is more than math. More importantly, EDUCATION teaches you who you are and whose you are.

He should have told me that reading should be similar to eating, done daily and consuming the best. He should have told me that leaders are readers and readers become leaders.

The more I reflect on my EDUCATION or my lack of EDUCATION, it makes me realize that there's no legitimate reason why I should not have gone on and attained a master's degree, or even a Ph.D.

No one told me that in most cases your level of EDUCATION determines your level of income. As I think about my EDUCATION and growing up on the South Side of Chicago, I can remember only two male teachers that intentionally helped me excel pertaining to my EDUCATION.

There was one male teacher during my elementary years and one male teacher during my high school years. Mr. Cross was one of my high school teachers who taught business math. Whenever my mother came to the school to check on my progress, she would always talk with Mr. Cross and then share what he said about me.

She told me things like: Mr. Cross said that you are good in math and that you should take it seriously. Even though I kept it a secret, I admired Mr. Cross to the point that I wanted to be just like him. I never forgot how Mr. Cross would dress when he was at school. He would always have on a double-breasted suit, shirt, and a tie with a matching pocket square.

Mr. Cross would wear a pair of wire framed glasses, you know the one's that make you look smart. He drove a two-seated Fiat, it was tan, and had a beautiful brown ragtop. I described his car because I've always wanted to own one just like his.

In my neighborhood and amongst my friends, the only person I can think of who went to college before me or after me for that matter, was my friend, David Henson. David was dating my cousin Cathy Key and it was my senior year in high school when David asked me "Clean (my neighborhood name) what college are you going to?

I looked at him reluctantly and then he asked, "have you taken your ACT? David was the only male to ever ask me that question, and he was only a year older than me. My daddy should have asked me what college I was going to! More importantly, my daddy should have had me prepared to take the ACT.

In fact, as I think about my EDUCATION or my lack of, I can remember that I had never even been on a college campus or even talked to a college student. As a matter of fact, it was when I was taking the ACT where the school counselor asked the question, "where would you like your test scores to be sent?" I replied, "Harvard, Yale, the University of Chicago and Jarvis Christian College."

Unbeknownst to her, I had no idea where I wanted to send my ACT scores. I had never visited a college campus. I never knew anyone who attended or was in college. As a matter of fact, the only reason I included Jarvis Christian College among the list of potential colleges was because my girlfriend's sister stated that's where she attended the night before I took the ACT.

I arrived at Jarvis Christian College on September 10, 1979, two weeks past late registration. I thank God that I was accepted. The registration personnel asked me "What is your desired major and minor, and what is your denomination?" I ambiguously replied, "I don't play dominos."

My daddy should have told me what was meant by collegiate field of studies and religious affiliations. I can attest that I struggled tremendously through high school as well as college. I wish I had a male example to show me the importance of a solid EDUCATION.

I went to college to simply be different. I perceived myself as being a person like Mr. Cross. Simply put, I wanted to be proud, self-confident (not to be mistaken with arrogance) and an empowering, motivational leader.

I had no idea of all the opportunities that can be available having a college degree. On the other hand, a higher educational degree does not automatically make you smart, but it does indicate that you have completed a daunting educational achievement that can never be taken away from you.

Hence, I have learned and shared with countless others that there are numerous benefits pertaining to acquiring a college degree. Most notably, a college degree has value that states you are educated. More importantly, a college degree is worth the time, effort, stress and the cost.

The most vital point that people think of pertaining to attaining an educational degree is to increase your earning potential. Numerous studies have concluded that obtaining a college degree will more than likely earn you more money throughout your career than only having a high school education.

Second, attaining a college degree will strengthen your marketability as a job seeker. There is an abundant amount of literature that I was taught in college. Yet, most of it I cannot recall or decipher automatically. However, I can attest that I have improved in terms of having a better character, discipline, way of life, and a greater ability to think analytically. These few reasons alone are primarily what top notch fortune 500 company employers seek pertaining to college graduates when looking to fill job positions.

College degrees make people marketable and create a better opportunity for career goals and options. On the other hand, high school graduates have to seek entry-level positions or non-skilled positions, which in most cases will include longer work hours, physical labor, and lesser wages and benefits.

Therefore, earning a college degree whether bachelors or associates, will open doors of employment and career opportunities that could otherwise be shut.

Also, skills that are accumulated by earning a college degree provide a multitude of networking opportunities that may be inaccessible to those who don't go to college.

Third, numerous investigations have shown that college graduates are more likely to receive greater employee benefits than employees without a college degree. In today's times, this is especially true when it comes to healthcare coverage.

Additionally, college graduates have greater opportunities to receive tuition reimbursement, health savings accounts, retirement matching, free or reduced childcare, and reimbursement for travel or commuting costs. In fact, I have witnessed in some instances where a benefits package can be worth almost as much as an employee's actual take-home pay.

Fourth, various research has determined that college graduates are typically more satisfied with their careers than individuals with a high school diploma. I once heard a person state, "find the type of work that you like doing and that way you don't mind doing your job."

When most people spend almost their entire lives working, job satisfaction can be a huge factor in overall satisfaction with life as well as a sense of well-being. Equally important, various investigations have shown that as your level of education increases, so does the level of job satisfaction.

Hence, college graduates are typically more satisfied with their careers than non-college graduates for numerous reasons. In most cases, they're able to find higher paying employment opportunities, apply for positions that offer job advancement opportunities, get hired by companies that provide generous benefits, and are able to work in fields and industries that interest them.

Fifth, college degrees may also lead to greater job stability. For example, during an economic plunge within the nation, it's not uncommon for companies to layoff or even cut jobs. I have personally witnessed the positions that are first to get cut. In most cases, it is the employees that are at the bottom or entry level positions, or have general skills that require unskilled labor.

During an economic recession, the unemployment rate among college graduates is always substantially lower than the unemployment rate among employees with only a high school diploma.

Sixth, acquiring a college degree can have a direct impact as well as numerous benefits for your children. Not only are children of parents with a college education better off socially and economically, but various research has shown that children in households where one or both parents have a college degree are themselves more likely to earn a college degree. Hence, earning a college degree can have a ripple effect that will influence the well-being of your immediate family as well as generations to come.

Next, you have the flexibility to make better choices. For example, a college education helps individuals to think critically, to decipher and solve problems with less information when dealing with complex issues.

Lastly, a college degreed individual has the ability to communicate more effectively. In most cases, college degreed individuals have better written and verbal communication skills than individuals with only a high school diploma. In fact, I believe that of all the benefits provided by earning a college degree, this is the most valuable. For example, communication skills influence just about every aspect of your life.

There is a multitude of benefits that verbal and written communication provides. The ability to communicate clearly, concisely, and persuasively will help you land the perfect job, improve your career advancement opportunities and enhance your interpersonal relationships with family members and associates.

Attaining a college associate degree usually takes two years, and four years for a bachelor's degree, six years for a master's degree, and eight years for a doctorate degree. I realize and honestly believe now that every man should have a Ph.D. It only takes an average of eight adult years. There is an African proverb that states, "He who is intelligent and no longer seeks to be intelligent is no longer intelligent."

For the men that are reading this book, please go and get your degree. It may not make you smarter, but it may make your life much richer and easier physically, socially, financially and emotionally.

What My Daddy Should Have Told Me About Education

- "The job of the conscious is to make the unconscious conscious." ~Kwame Ture

- "Education makes a people easy to lead, but difficult to drive; easy to govern but impossible to enslave." (*unknown*)

- "Children learn from what you are more than what you teach." (Unknown)

- "If you think education is expensive, try ignorance" (Unknown)

- "Education is the most powerful weapon we can use to change the world." ~Nelson Mandela

- It does not matter how slowly you go as long as you do not stop. ~Confucius

- "Once you have an education no one can take it away." (Unknown)

CHAPTER 3

WHAT MY DADDY SHOULD HAVE TOLD ME ABOUT MY HISTORY

What is culture? Webster defines culture as, "The beliefs, customs, arts, etc. of a particular society, group, place, or time." I have heard the expression, "It's only when you begin your HISTORY in a state of freedom that you will come to properly understand your role in life." All Africans born in America who begin their HISTORY in 1619 may never solve our people's problems. In order to solve our people's problems we must begin at the origin of our HISTORY in Africa.

It was only when I began to study MY HISTORY that my life began to change. As a matter of fact, studying My-HISTORY lured me closer to God. It was then that I picked up the Bible and began to study and learn.

Through the study of MY HISTORY I learned that the Garden of Eden happened to be in Africa. That was amazing to me; it was an eye opening experience. I remember that moment all so well. It was at Jarvis Christian College when one of my instructors made the comment that the Garden of Eden was in Africa. He talked about the rivers that surrounded the Garden of Eden and stated that all of those rivers are in the continent of Africa. (Genesis 2:10)

From then on I began to ask questions and I began to study My-HISTORY. My daddy should have told me about the importance of MY HISTORY.

As I began to study about MY HISTORY I became more responsible, my grades improved, and even my manners improved. As a matter of fact, my whole life improved.

I remember back in college when my roommate, Michael Hayes gave me a poem by Nikki Giovanni, "Ego Tripping." I memorized that poem in one day and it has been with me ever since. One year when I came home from school, I remember my Aunt Bonney saying, "Oh Lord they got him, the boys dressed like an African!"

Once I became rooted in my true African culture things began to change. It was as if I did not fit in anymore with friends, acquaintances, and relatives I used to hang around. For example, I wouldn't hang around the drug dealers, gangsters, and fathers who were not being fathers and the mothers who were not being mothers. At times I would spend all day just reading. I would absorb knowledge from book after book.

I was reading so much until one day my son "Rikki Man" said, "Daddy why are you reading all of those books?" I simply replied, "Son, reading needs to be like eating done daily and consuming the best."

Everyone in my family could see the positive changes that were now instilled within my character.

When I officially moved to Texas, I read a book called the Browder Files by Anthony T. Browder. This book consisted of 22 essays about "Africans born in America"(African Americans).

After reading that book I would then read the referenced books. I wanted to know the author's frame of reference. You know, "Where did he get this information from?"

When I moved to Arlington, Texas, I made acquaintances with a friend named George Woods. George was attending the University of Texas at Arlington. George was a young African man who was originally from Africa.

Once, I went to his house to borrow a suitcase for my trip back home to Chicago. When I got to his house there was this guy there trying to sale him some books about Africa. I was in a hurry and it seemed like this guy was really trying to get George to buy the books, but George was not interested. So I told the guy "Look I'm in a hurry. I have a flight to catch, I need to get this suitcase and get out of here so I don't miss my plane!" Then I said, "I'll tell you what, let me buy all the books." It was at this point in my life that I began to study about "Rites of Passage" because one of the books written by Jawanza Kunjufue tackled this topic.

For those of you that aren't familiar with the "Rites of Passage," this is a tradition borrowed from our ancestors in Africa. In Africa, boys and girls have to complete their "Rites of Passage" to become a man or woman.

Another book that I purchased was titled "*Vision for the Black Man* by Naima Akbar." After reading Akbar's book, I had to ask my girlfriend to move out. Why you might ask? It was in this book that I learned, "boys play house, but men get married." During this time in my life I was definitely not ready to get married, so she had to move out. The next day I made a call to Chicago and asked the mothers of my boys to send them to me, because it was simply time to "man up."

As I reflect back on the information that was given to me as a child, I never recalled any male ever talking to me about my HISTORY.

No one told me that my ancestors were architects and engineers of the highest order. They did not tell me that our ancestors taught Plato, Pythagoras and Socrates. No one ever shared My-HISTORY with me. The only thing I was ever told about my HISTORY was that my ancestors were slaves.

No one ever shared with me that my ancestors gave the world the concept of time. From seconds to minutes, minutes to hours, hours to days, days to weeks, weeks to months and months to years. No one shared with me, that we gave the world the first calendar.

No one shared with me that we created the great pyramid that sits in the center of the earth, is 48 stories high, 755 feet wide, taking 2,300,000 stones to build, is still standing today and has not been duplicated. The chief architect is a Black man named Imhotep. He was also the first doctor, first mathematician and chief builder of the step pyramid.

No one shared with me that my ancestors taught the world reading, writing and math. No one shared with me that we established the first university in the world. It was called Luxor, and it was located in Egypt.

Did you know that Egypt is in Africa? It is not the Middle East. You can't take a country out of a continent and call it the Middle East. If there is a Middle East then there has to be a Middle West a Middle North and a Middle South. No, Egypt is in the continent of Africa.

No one shared with me, our ancestors were mapping out the celestial stars while other people were still in their caves.

My daddy should have told me about MY HISTORY

My daddy should have told me, that it was my ancestors who gave the world the concept of one God. It was my ancestors who gave the world the concept of the Trinity.

I will never forget when I was young, I had to be around 10 or 11, because I was still in elementary school. We had a chance to go to the University of Chicago's

Oriental Institute. I remember seeing the mummies and the statues of Black people and I knew they were Black. But I was always taught something different. I was taught that the Egyptians were white.

I don't know if you remember it or not, but there was a movie called Indiana Jones and the Temple of Doom. It was based on an archaeologist from the University of Chicago. The guy who played the character in the movie is Harrison Ford. I mention this, because in the movie you will see the Egyptians were always white. It was the same in the movie "The Ten Commandments." They portrayed the Egyptians and the people in Africa as all white, when in reality these people were Black. There is evidence to support this.

My daddy should have told me about MY HISTORY.

I sit and wonder what my life would have been like if my daddy would have told me about my story when I was young, like back in kindergarten. I could have absorbed all of the great things my ancestors did from the time I was in kindergarten, to middle school to high school to graduating from college. Imagine what my life would have been like if MY HISTORY, was taught to me like his-story has been taught to me.

I can only imagine what my life would have been like, if I was taught my story for 11 months out of the year, and his-story one month out of the year. And let his-story be the shortest month of the year, the coldest month of the year and have to share it with Groundhog Day, Valentine's Day and Presidents' Day.

My daddy should have told me about MY HISTORY

But I'll tell you when I did learn about MY HISTORY my whole life changed. I started loving God more. As I began to learn MY HISTORY I started loving me more and loving my people more. I began to want to be a responsible father, a loving husband and an encouraging dad. I wanted to educate my children and the children around them.

You might be asking why is it, so important to know your HISTORY.

Knowing your history and culture gives you a sense of accomplishment. You feel a sense of pride and you believe that you too can accomplish great things.

My Daddy Should Have Told Me
About My History

- "You don't have to burn books to destroy a culture. Just get people to stop reading." (Unknown)

- "The Black skin is not a badge of shame, but rather a glorious symbol of national greatness." ~Marcus Garvey

- "Never compromise your culture, because you are your culture." (Unknown)

- "The color of the skin is in no way connected with strength of the mind or intellectual powers." ~Benjamin Banneker

- "I am African not because I was born in Africa, but because Africa is born in me." (Unknown)

- Slavery is not African history, Slavery is an interruption of African History. (Unknown)

- "People say that slaves were taken from Africa. This is not true. People were taken from Africa and were made into slaves." (Unknown)

CHAPTER 4

WHAT MY DADDY SHOULD HAVE TOLD ME ABOUT CHILD SUPPORT

I had my first child when I was 16 years old and I didn't really know what to do. I will never forget when my son's grandfather, Mr. Wright came to me and said, "So you and my daughter are having a baby. When are you getting married?" I started running and crying and ran to my granddaddy. At this time, I didn't even know my father. My granddaddy said "You don't have to get married, but you do have to take care of the baby for the rest of your life."

Right then reality set in. I can remember clearly. I was a junior in high school, telling my friends that I'm about to have a baby. No one even believed me. On June 30, 1978 my first son was born. "Rikki Man" is what we called him and at that point I didn't know what to do. I started thinking about my own dad and how he was not there for me. The one thing I did know was that I would not do that to my son. The thought occurred to me, how was I going to take care of a son when I couldn't even take care of myself? My mother was on AFDC (After Daddy Cut Out) you know, the food stamps program.

We were living like in the movie *Lackawanna Blues*. We were living with my grandmother, aunt, uncle and their kids. The house was packed and just around the corner I had a little son now dependent upon me. His mother named him Rikki Rashaad Wright, not Junior or little Rickie, because she was mad at me for not being at the hospital the day he was born. At the time I didn't know my custodial rights, so she was able to make decisions without asking any advice from me. It was at this point that she put me on child support. She did not know what she was doing and I did not know what I was doing.

Chicago law states if you get public assistance you have to give the name of the father. I tell you, if you want to find someone, put them on child-support. They may not find them for the IRS, but they will find them for child-support.

Now I was only 17 years old and jobless. So I did what I thought would be in the best interest for my child and enrolled in college. I thought that if I wanted more for my son I would need more skills. With no job and on my way to college, I had no idea that for every month I missed a child-support payment, not only the payment, but the fees were also piling up against me. By the time I graduated from college, I had child support for a second son, Ashley "Thirsty" as well.

So let's do the math. That means upon graduation I had college debt, plus child support for two children and no job. When I graduated I had to go back home and live with my grandmother, uncle, aunts and by this time their kids had kids. When I returned home from college, I felt like I had the whole world on my shoulders.

My Daddy Should Have Told Me About Child Support

I remember my first job after I graduated from college with a degree in mathematics. I worked at a grocery store called "One Stop Foods and Grocery." I was a stamper (the person who put the stamped prices on the canned goods). I also had a second job at UPS. As a matter of fact I got fired from UPS because I couldn't read the addresses on the boxes fast enough. That's when I learned I needed glasses. But I was not able to purchase them due to a lack of finances. You see child support was taken out beginning with my very first check. I was only making nine dollars an hour on one job and seven dollars an hour on the other.

My Daddy Should Have Told Me About Child Support

My Daddy or some man should have told me "don't make a baby until you're able to afford one." If you're reading this book, I advise you not to have any children until you are financially and emotionally able to support them. When and if you decide to have children, know that you will be responsible for them the rest of your life.

Some people always try to comprehend why so many brothers have several kids (or seeds planted) with different women and then complain about how much they are paying every month in child support. I'm pretty sure that they were not thinking about these financial obligations when they were seeking a variety of women looking for sex. Or in other words, maybe they were letting their "little head think for their big head."

And then what about the women who let men into their lives knowing that he is no good but then get angry because he is a deadbeat dad? A lot of these people experience this at a young age, however it is still an undesirable cycle that has continuously plagued the African American community.

One of the easiest ways for an African American man to continually struggle financially in life is to pay ongoing child support. The downside to this is that a great percentage of African American men don't think about the consequences of having and raising children. When you have kids at an early age, you can't necessarily move forward as easily later on. You might decide, "Oh now I'm ready to get married and have a family," but guess what? You still have obligations from previous relationships that you have to fulfill financially and that can be troublesome. It's been said that children are a gift from God, what we make of our children is a gift to God.

For every young man reading this book, I suggest that you choose wisely when you decide to have children. Not only will that child be a part of your life but so will the mother of that child. Choose wisely.

If the relationship with the mother of your child does not work out, don't be angry and don't take it out on the child. Don't become bitter, become better. I really dislike it when mothers who don't get what they wanted out of the relationship, begin to talk bad about the father to the children.

Don't get me wrong I am not against child support. I just believe that child support is more than just financial support. I believe that a father should be there for his child emotionally and spiritually as well. A father should bond with his child by spending quality time, not just weekend visits. He should attend birthday parties and sporting events once the child is of age. The father should be there to lead and guide the child on this journey of life with love and understanding.

What I don't like about child support is the way the system is set up. I didn't like the idea of not being given the chance to take care of my children before being taken to court. I felt violated when I was put on child support by a system that is set-up to destroy the Black family. I felt like my children were treated like assets and that they were the sole property of their mothers and I had no say so in the matter.

What My Daddy Should Have Told Me
about Child Support

- "Your first obligation as a parent is to not bring chaos into your kids' lives." ~Dr. Laura.com
- The average child support payment made in the U.S. is $430 a month.
- There are no national guidelines for determining an adequate amount of child support. Each state uses its own calculations to set child support payments.
- Child support and visitation rights are two distinct and different legal matters. (You can't legally stop paying child support just because an ex makes it hard for you or even prevents you from seeing your child).
- Child support is not dischargeable by bankruptcy. (Even if you are dead broke, deep in debt or out of work, a bankruptcy judge cannot wipe out due or past due child support payments).
- A parent who is unemployed or has a reduction in income is still required to pay all court-ordered child support, unless that parent has received a court-approved, written child support modification from a judge.
- Failure to pay child support can lead to serious consequences, including wage garnishment, asset seizure, credit bureau reporting, driver's license suspension, passport denial, withholding of unemployment benefits, and even arrest or jail time.

CHAPTER 5
MY DADDY SHOULD HAVE TOLD ME ABOUT WHAT TO DO WHEN STOPPED BY THE POLICE

As I previously stated I was born on the Southeast side of Chicago, where we see the police all the time. As a matter of fact we see the police just like we see the bus - every 15 minutes. I remember growing up on the Southeast side seeing other people get stopped by a policeman or harassed by the police, but honestly until I graduated with a college degree I had never had an encounter with the police.

I will never forget my first encounter with the police. I was riding the bus from 79th and King Drive to 75th and Cottage Grove. I saw the 75th Street bus coming, at this time there was a Black man standing next to me and as he was standing next to me two officers or two guys in an unmarked car, said something to the guy. I asked him, "are you ok, bro? He said, "I'm cool."

To my astonishment, rather than confronting the guy at the bus stop, the two white officers grabbed me and pulled me off as I stepped onto the bus. They put me into the car and took me around to an alley. They pulled me out of the car and put me up against a garage door.

I remember being very scared. I thought they were going to kill me. He said "don't you know we're the police?" I was like, "yeah." He then stated, "well the next time you see two white guys in a Black community we're either the police or were coming to buy some pussy."

One of them then looked into my wallet. I gave him my ID and my pocket diploma showing that I had just graduated from Jarvis Christian College. He looks at the degree and says "we will let you make it this time. But remember, the next time you see two white officers or two white men in a Black community, we are either police or only coming to buy pussy." He gave me my wallet back and drove off. I was so upset, that I walked all the way home and it was a very long walk from 75th and Cottage Grove to 75th and Coles. But it gave me time to think and try to process what had just happened to me. I asked myself, why did this happen?

At the time I was working in a summer program for the City of Chicago. I was placed at the 3rd District Police Department which was located on 75th and Cottage Grove. On the walk home after the incident with the police, I had to walk past the police station where I worked. Until that day I thought I wanted to be a policeman, but this incident made changed that dream.

My second encounter with the police happened when I moved to Fort Worth, Texas. I had my sons in the car and I was driving through a small suburb called Pantego, Texas.

I was driving down Rosedale which turns into 303 going east from Fort Worth when I was pulled over. The police officer was talking kind of harsh to me. My verbal responses were simply "yes sir, no sir and how can I help you sir." He asked for my license and my insurance. I said "sir, I'm going into my wallet to give you my license and I'm reaching in my glove compartment to give you my insurance card, sir." He said "thank you." I said "no thank you, sir." I gave him my license and he went back to his car. My son asked, "Daddy why you being all nice? You don't have to be nice to him."

I said "son, you are right, I might beat the ticket but I'm not going to beat a drive down to the police station a place I don't want to go." It's always better to be respectful even when you're being disrespected.

My Daddy Should Have Told Me About The Police

My third encounter with the police happened during the time I was running for a seat on the Fort Worth City Council. I had lost the race but I was contesting the count.

I was driving home with my campaign treasurer Frederick Darden II in the passenger seat. We were about two blocks from my house when the police pulled up behind me. Fred said, "Rick the police are behind you." I said, "they are probably reading my license plates. I don't have any tickets. I let the police do their job and I do my job."

By now I'm a block away from my house when the police turns on his lights. "I said, oh man what is he stopping me for?" By this time I am on the block where I live. I decided to pull up into my driveway and I let the garage up to indicate that I lived there.

I was getting out of the car when the police officer rushed up to the car pushed me back into the car and he slams the door back! He says "get back in the car. You know what happened to RaRa." I said, "What did you just say?" He repeated, "Don't you know what happened to RaRa? Don't you get out of that car." I looked at Fred silently saying, look how they treat us.

Charal "RaRa" Thomas was a young man shot by the police on February 28, 2011 about a month before they stopped me. He had his three minor children in the car ages 11, 8 and 7. The police shot him several times killing him in the presence of his three children. The official report said he was evading arrests. The officer involved was not charged.

After I gave the police officer my driver's license and insurance and he went back to his car, two other police cars pulled up to my driveway with their lights on. By this time my neighbors began to come out. They all witnessed this incident.

After the police officer brought back my ID and driver's license, I asked, "can I now get out the car?" He said, "Yes, you can get out of the car." Fred and I get out of the car and I say to the police officer, "Why would you say that to me about RaRa?" He said, "What did you say? I said, why did you say that to me about RaRa?" He said "Go and tell the other officer what you said." I walked over to the other police officer and said "Sir, the other officer told me to ask you why would he say that to me about RaRa?"

At this point the police officer grabs me and pins me up against the car. He put his arm on my neck and started choking me, telling me he can arrest me. I said "Then arrest me. I haven't done anything wrong." All my neighbors are looking. Everybody's looking. They began screaming and hollering for the police to release me. I said, "let me go. I haven't done anything."

He released me and I ran into my garage. The other policeman started walking towards me, but then suddenly stopped and he said "let's go." It was as if they had seen something. I looked back in my garage and there was a sign that said, Vote Rickie Clark City Council District Five. Yes, they were harassing Rickie Clark, who was running as a candidate for the Fort Worth City Council! That let me know if they would do it to me, a potential City Councilman, imagine what they would do to other African-Americans that live in the community?

My Daddy Should Have Told Me About The Police

Now don't get me wrong, I have the utmost respect for the profession but not for all cops. I have a few friends who are policemen. My son's stepfather, Dwayne Betts is a police officer. My best friend Bert Lewis, was a police officer, Luther Perry and Donnell Ross, friends of mine were also police officers. My boys, Chuck and Bird from Detroit are police officers. My main man Clyde Franklin,

"Officer Franklin" as the kids call him, who has been down with me since I moved to Fort Worth, Texas is also an officer. As a matter of fact, Clyde would babysit my son's and play Sony PlayStation. So I have no disrespect for police officers, especially when they are wearing the badge for real.

My Daddy Should Have Told Me About The Police

What to Do If Stopped While Driving

- Pull over safely to the side of the road if you see a police car with flashing lights behind you.
- If the officer asks where you're from, politely ask why you were stopped—the Supreme Court has ruled that the officer must have a reasonable suspicion based on "specific and articulable facts" that a person is armed or has committed, is committing, or is about to commit a crime.
- Answer the officer's questions as succinctly as possible, without embellishment.
- Always have your identification handy; if the officer asks for your license and registration, get his permission to reach for them—you don't want him thinking you may be reaching for a weapon.
- If they ask for permission to search your car, politely refuse.
- If the officer tells you to get out of the car, do as he says—and if he puts you up against the car, stay there.
- If the police insist on searching the vehicle, remain silent while they are doing so.
- Most importantly–though you will certainly be outraged—don't give the cop any attitude, or any reason to claim you were hostile or difficult, because that's the quickest way to escalate the encounter.

What To Do If Stopped While Walking

- No matter what, never run from the police.
- Police have the right to stop you and ask your name, so if this happens, politely tell them your name.
- Beyond that initial question, remember the US Constitution guarantees each of us the right to remain silent, so don't volunteer any additional information.
- Because the stop is usually a pretext for the officer to have close contact with you to see if you are under the influence of alcohol or illegal drugs, or in possession of contraband, be as polite and courteous as possible.
- Don't curse or antagonize the officer.
- There is a good chance the officer is stopping you because he believes you match the description from a suspect who did something nearby—such as a young Black male with short hair. If that's the case, you won't be able to talk your way out of it—so don't say anything.

What To Do If Arrested

- Be polite and don't contradict the officer's reason for arresting you.
- Try to stay calm and resist the urge to become loud or aggressive.
- Use every ounce of your willpower to resist the urge to say something to get them to release you—it's not going to happen, and will likely just make things worse.
- As soon as you can, call someone who can hire you an attorney to come to the station as soon as possible.
- If your parents or family members come to assist you, resist the urge to explain to them everything that happened –the police are likely recording every word you say to them.

What To Do If You See Police Harassing a Friend

- Don't confront the police.
- Your primary job is to get your friend to remain as calm and nonthreatening as possible. Keep telling him, "calm down and be quiet."
- Create some distance between you and police so they don't perceive you as dangerous.
- As surreptitiously as possible, turn on the recording device on your cell phone. Having a video or audio recording of the encounter may become extremely important.
- Do not intervene, because there's nothing you can do except escalate the encounter and make it worse.
- Make sure you get the badge number of the officer involved.

(A version of this list first appeared in the November 2013 issue of Ebony magazine)

"Sometimes you just have to close your eyes, count to ten, take a deep breath, remind yourself that you wouldn't look good in prison stripes and just smile at that person and walk away."

CHAPTER 6

WHAT MY DADDY SHOULD HAVE TOLD ME ABOUT MONEY

I am not necessarily the person to speak on this subject; but the other day my son Ashley aka "Thirsty" came in the house and said, "Dad you need to write about finances, because I don't know anything about saving money. I said, "son you're talking to the wrong person, because not one male, not one boy, not one man ever told me about finances, money or what to do with money."

There were no men around my house talking about finance. The men I knew carried their money in their pockets. As a matter of fact my mother's idea of saving money was taking her change and putting it behind the couch. I did learn how to save change but I never really knew how to save money.

My Daddy Should Have Told Me About Money

While I feel I may not be the person to write on this subject, it is a very important subject that needs to be taught to young men everywhere. So with that being said, let me just share my experience on money with you.

First let's define money. Webster defines money as a medium of exchange. For example most of us go to a job every day. We give them our time and energy in exchange for their money. When we go to the store we give them our money that we have earned in exchange for merchandise, shoes, clothes, groceries, etc.

My Daddy Should Have Told Me About Money

There is a Scripture in the Bible: 1st Timothy 6:10, that is often misquoted. They say, the Bible says that money is the root of all evil. Let's correct that right now. The Bible says that, "The LOVE of money is the root of all evil." Money itself is neither good nor bad, it is simply a medium of exchange.

Some people love money so much that they will do anything to obtain it. A lot of people get in trouble going after this thing called money. But I'm here to tell you differently. If you pursue your purpose with passion the money will come. You won't have to chase it, it will chase you. As a matter of fact I challenge you. Find something you love doing so much that you would do it for free, but become so good at it that you get paid for it.

Reflecting on my upbringing, money wasn't something that was talked about in my family. No one ever talked about saving money or how to invest your money so that it works for you and not the other way around. Almost everyone in my family was living paycheck to paycheck. Nobody had any real money.

When I was in college, my idea of having money was having food stamps. (Back in the day in Chicago, they used to come in little books, you had the $5 book, the $10 book, and they were different colors.) This is what my mother would send me when I told her I needed money while in college. Back then my idea of having money was more so in what you had that could be seen, rather than what you had in the bank that couldn't be seen.

If you drove a nice car, wore nice clothing and shoes, then I thought you had money. To me money was what you spent not what you saved. I remember cashing my check and keeping all my money in my pocket. The thought never occurred to me that I should save some for a rainy day. I would always say, save for what? I was living my life day by day. I never considered a rainy day, getting older or retirement. I think I was around 28 years old before I got my first checking account.

My Daddy Should Have Told Me About Money

I'm telling you I had no clue about money. Even well into my late 20's and early 30's earning around $60K a year, I still didn't understand the concept of money. I had no understanding of a 401(k), IRA, CD's or Mutual Funds. It wasn't until I met my current CPA and friend, Roy Paley that any man ever talked to me about money and what I should be doing with it.

You see Roy did my taxes and he saw the money I was making. One day he sat me down and talked to me about saving and investing. At this point bad habits had already been formed and they would be hard to break. I also had a friend, Jeff Jones, who would talk to me about saving money as well. I should have listened to them, but I was too busy living life.

I remember Roy telling me the things that his father had taught him about money. He taught him how to be responsible with his money and not spend it all on flashy things. His dad even made him pay his way through college. Roy graduated without owing any student loans, because he had a dad schooling him about money. He said that his mother and father told him that if he made any babies, he would have to move out and take care of them. Roy never had any kids. Even to this day he has no kids.

My Daddy Should Have Told Me About Money

It takes money to live, however you should never spend all that you own, trying to look good. You should always pay yourself first. At least 10% of your paycheck should go into a savings account or better yet a mutual fund, every payday. You should always have on hand at least three months of living expenses. Let's say you're living expenses total $3,000 a month. You should always have $9,000 tucked away in a saving account somewhere that you can't touch. This is strictly your emergency account.

If the company you work for has a 401(k) plan where they match dollar for dollar or a certain percentage, always take full advantage of that. You should also learn about mutual funds, CD's and government bonds. Mutual Funds can grow your money faster than a regular savings account. Make sure your portfolio is diversified. You have heard the saying, "Don't put all your eggs in one basket." As soon as you can, invest in real estate. I think every man should own their first piece of property by at least age 30. It can be a condo, house or apartment building, but own something.

You should only have one major credit card. Credit is a dangerous thing if you aren't disciplined in your finances. It is easy to buy now and pay later. You will always spend more on credit than you will if you had cash. It is so important to keep your credit in good standings. If you do charge, make sure you pay more than the minimum payment and please pay on time.

Your credit score will determine how much you pay for everything from a home to life insurance. So whatever you do please make sure that you keep your credit in high standings.

What My Daddy Should Have Told Me
About Money

- Do not save what is left after spending, but spend what is left after saving. ~Warren Buffett

- Money looks better in the bank than on your feet. (Unknown)

- The man who does more than he is paid, will soon be paid for more than he does. (Unknown)

- Too many people spend money they haven't earned, to buy things they don't want, to impress people they don't like. ~Will Smith

- When it comes to money ignorance is not bliss. What you don't know can hurt you. (Unknown)

- Create a budget and stick to it. (Unknown)

- Pay your debts as soon as possible, your word is bond. (Unknown)

CHAPTER 7

WHAT MY DADDY SHOULD HAVE TOLD ME ABOUT MANHOOD

I'm sure you have heard it said to a lot of boys, "Act like a man," but if you are anything like me and most of the young Black boys I grew up around, we were never shown what that looks like. I believe if I took one year to tour the country and ask the question, What does act like a man look like? I would probably get as many answers to this question as the number of boys that I asked.

So I ask the question, "What is a man"? I have been asking this question for quite some time now. I am a youth motivational speaker and I have had the opportunity to speak to youth from elementary to high school to college. It never fails when I make the statement, "I want all the men in the room to stand up." 95% of the males in the room will stand up.

So I ask the question again with emphasis on men, "I want all the men in the room to remain standing," and this time some of the males, recognizing that they are not men, will begin to sit down. I then ask the question "How do you know you are a man?" to the males who remain standing.

You won't believe some of the answers that I get or maybe you will. I get answers like "Because I have a mustache, "I just know I am a man, or "My momma told me I was a man." One of my all-time favorite responses is "Because I have a penis between my legs." That's when I let each and every one of them know a dog also has a penis between his legs. I also let them know that having a penis doesn't make you a man it makes you a male. That's right all men are males, but not all males are men.

I honestly empathize with each and every one of these young males. I know that if someone would have asked me that same question in my youth I would have given the same response. I tell you I've heard and believed those responses as a child. Now that I am a man I understand that "in order to be a man, you must see a man."

I can't speak for everyone else, but I can speak for myself on what I saw. I know that growing up without a responsible father or man greatly affected my life. I believe I can say the same for most of the males in the community where I grew up. We had very few positive men, mentors or role models to show us what it took to be a man. There was no clear definition of a man. We did not have Rites of Passage or Bar Mitzvahs. For me and most of my friends, we were never given the definition of a man.

Now Webster defines manhood as: *the state or condition of being an adult man and no longer a boy.*For the purposes of this book I am defining man as: *A male who acts, thinks and lives responsibly.*

I remember going to college and pledging Alpha Phi Alpha, a male fraternity. The tag line for Alpha's is "let us make man." I pledged for six weeks, to be made a man and I tell you it was one of the most profound things I did towards manhood. During my pledge period I was taught things like the importance of education, integrity, brotherhood, the love for all mankind, and the list goes on. I tell you the truth, it was my pledging of Alpha Phi Alpha that put me on my quest to manhood.

So what's the problem you ask? Over the years the message to boys about what it means to be a man has been truly confusing to say the least. We mistake the machismo of the street gangs for courage. Boys fill the vacancy left by missing fathers with video games, television, and music. The entertainment industry by way of films, glorifies male characters who refuse to grow up (*Baby Boy*) or confuses you (*Empire*) to a point that you don't know what a man is.

Our boys must weed through all these different and conflicting signals to figure out what it means to be a man and for many of them it is impossible to figure out. Unlike women, who have a lot of the principles of growing up and accepting responsibility instilled or forced on them when they are young girls, males normally grow up playing and will continue to play unless they decide to learn to develop into a man. It is important as males that we learn the necessary principles of being a man. A lot of the young men that I have worked with don't know how to answer the question "what is a man?" ... and they end up settling for a "less-than" life. They don't have a compelling manhood vision that is bigger and more meaningful than the conventional manhood that much of the world seems to be chasing; i.e. money, fame and sex. Many grown males lack clarity about what it truly means to be a man. As a result many boys are in a state of denial and are confused about manhood. Most young males find themselves competing and comparing themselves with what they see on the big screen and fail to learn about manhood. Most males end up disappointed with life, because most males compete with males.

My major strategy for this book is to assist young men in understanding that, regardless of their situation in life, they should assume the major responsibility for their own destiny.

Young men must also understand and, perhaps, hear us who are men admit that many adults will disappoint them. They don't intend to, but they will. Parents, educators, politicians and policemen are part of a special list of adults that can be disappointing to young men. But adults don't always behave fairly or have all of the necessary answers to the complexity of problems facing young men today.

Young men must understand that all decisions have consequences. Some consequences are major, some minor, some temporary, some permanent, but the consequences are always the result of the decisions.

They must over stand that decisions are a part of life, a part of living, and will always be a part of us. Decisions, then, cannot be left to chance. Young men must learn to make positive decisions, to look for alternatives, to examine and think about their actions and reactions. They must know that decisions today will hold consequences, directly or indirectly, for their lives tomorrow.

My Daddy Should Have Told Me About Manhood

Somebody should have told me that boys play house and men get married. Somebody should have told me that boys sag their pants, but men pull them up. Somebody should have told me that boys have babies but men take care of them. Somebody should have told me that boys are told to take the garbage out; men see that the garbage is full and take it out. Somebody should have told me that boys make excuses for why it can't be done; men make solutions for getting it done. Somebody should have told me that boys one-night-them, while men wife them.

We can't simply love our son's into manhood, we must raise them into manhood. We must challenge our son's academically, emotionally and spiritually. We must encourage them to be the best they can be, because in this day and age this world wants to destroy Black boys. In this day and age somebody right now is looking at their test scores and determining how many jails they need to build, so that they have a recession proof investment.

Every male owes it to his family, friends, woman, wife and community to develop into a strong man with character and integrity with respect and honor for mankind.

My Daddy Should Have Told Me
About Manhood

- "If you never allow your child to experience failure and disappointment, they will not be equipped to handle adulthood." ~Unknown

- "I'm thankful for my struggle, because without it I wouldn't have stumbled across my strength" ~Unknown

- "Don't blame your behavior on someone else. You are 100% responsible no matter how bad you are feeling or what's happening in your life." ~Dr. Laura.com

- "Every father should remember that one day his son will follow his example instead of his advice." ~Unknown

- "Don't be scared to cut off jealous, hateful, disrespectful, and disloyal people. You're better off without them" ~Livelifehappy.com

- "A man's success has a lot to do with the kind of woman he chooses to have in his life." ~Unknown

- "It is easier to build strong children than to repair broken men." ~Frederick Douglass

CHAPTER 8
WHAT YOUR DADDY SHOULD TELL YOU
(USE THESE QUESTIONS TO BEGIN A DIALOGUE WITH YOUR DADDY NOW)

Interview your Daddy

1. I am the Son of...?

2. I am the Grandson of...?

3. I am the Father of...?

4. I am the Brother of...?

5. I am the Uncle of...?

6. I am the Friend of...?

7. I was born and raised in what town?

8. I attended_____ High School?

9. I attended _____College?

10. When I was young I loved to...?

11. What do you wish your daddy would have told you?

12. What are three things you are most proud of...?

13. What are three things you are least proud of...?

14. What did you like most about your dad?

15. What did you like least about your dad?

16. What did you like about your grandfather(s)?

17. What did you like least about your Grandfather(s)?

18. What does success look like?

19. What was your occupation when I was born?

20. What dreams did you let go?

21. Did you love my mother when I was born?

22. What time in your life did you man up?

23. What was the hardest part of parenting?

24. Do you believe in God?

25. What is the most important advice you can give me now?

26. What message do you want to leave for your grandchildren?

CHAPTER 9
Words from other Men

WHAT MY FATHER TAUGHT ME
ABOUT MY HERITAGE AND EDUCATION
~Jacinto Ramos, Jr.

*I've known and mentored Jacinto for over 20 years and I am now
mentoring his son. He is the current
Fort Worth Independent School District Board President*

As a father of 3 boys, I am blessed to have an amazing father set a high bar. I am the exception to the rule on this subject. I realize on a daily basis the importance of having a strong loving father as a certified Texas Juvenile Probation Officer, youth minister, FWISD School Board member, and TCU Adjunct Professor.

My father is from a border town in Mexico. He grew up in the streets of Ciudad Acuña, Coahuila. He is the kid my friends in college made fun of selling gum in the Plaza and shining shoes. I never found it amusing to laugh at children in poverty and even more so...of children robbed of a childhood. My father missed out on a childhood and a high quality education in order to help provide income for the home.

He violated Child Labor Laws by forcing me to work for Don Manuel in Diamond-Hill (DH) when I was 12 years old. DH is a neighborhood in Fort Worth, Texas. Working every summer until I turned 16 years of age were the most grueling years of my adolescent life. I worked side by side with men from Mexico that were undocumented. They were paid $150 a week and my father only allowed Don Manuel to pay me $50 a week. As you can imagine, I was very angry with my father for not allowing me to be paid the money I had rightfully earned. The first week at the age of 12 I asked him why he was doing this to me. The following is what my Apa (Daddy) told me:

"As a teenager, you do not need to have an excess of money. You will learn 3 things from working for Don Manuel:

1. You will learn the value of hard work

2. You will learn how to save your money and make it last

3. You will appreciate the value of an education

I do not want you to ever look down on your own people. Working side by side with undocumented men shows you that no human being can be illegal. You come from a people that works hard. I need you to work hard with your brain...not your hands."

Don Manuel and my father did not finish school in Mexico. They instilled in me a drive to work hard in school and motivated me to want an education to honor them.

Don Manuel showed up to my high school and college graduation events. Each time with an envelope filled with money totaling $500. He stated each time,

"Que orgullo nos das, bien hecho" as he laid his hand on my shoulder. He came to my wedding a year after graduating from college. He said the same words and told me the money was what he owed me for the years of hard work when my father didn't allow him to pay me.

As a father, I have taken these and many other lessons my father taught me. I have tried to do him justice by living my life in a manner that honors his name. You see, I'm a "Jr." and understand I belong to him. I have a Master's degree because he loved me, he taught me, and he validated me. I am proud to be of Mexican descent, I am proud to be his son, and I am proud to have 3 beautiful sons of my own. The baton has been passed and I am doing my absolute best to change the world...my 3 sons' world.

WHAT MY DADDY SHOULD HAVE TOLD ME ABOUT CHILD SUPPORT
~Charles D. Rousseau a/k/a "Mo"

*Charles Rousseau is a life-long friend from Jarvis Christian
College who taught me a lot about spirituality and religion based
on what he learned from his father. He is now
Commissioner District 5, Fayette County, Georgia*

Clearly my father neglected to tell me about the perils and challenges associated with child support. But then again, how could he have known? You see my father; long time pastor, family patriarch, highly respected community organizer, public policy hack with five children enjoyed married life with my mother for fifty-three years until his transition in 2009. I would venture to say from his couples/marriage counseling experiences he would have encountered one or two sessions where child support was a dynamic of the relationship.

While my dad and I enjoyed some lengthy discussions and debates about responsible sex, our discussions never broached the subject of child support in the event of an unplanned pregnancy. We did however talk about STD's but never the real aftermath of non-custodial parenting that required financial support. See I was nurtured and indoctrinated with the belief that sexual intercourse was to be reserved for marriage, yet I chose to experiment with unprotected sexual intercourse none the less.

Well, growing up in the late 70's and being inundated with messages of sexual freedom, it was hard to reconcile my parental message with the social/peer messages swirling around me. Brothers and sisters "if I knew then what I know now," I would have taken my father and mother at their word and avoided this painful condition. A condition that hurts all parties involved equally and without bias. All parties suffer the consequences of child support but the greatest bone chilling effects are reserved for the child.

For I have learned, children bear the indignities of having to figure out why their mother and father did not see fit to remain together after they we conceived and brought forth into this world. While growing up children cannot understand nor grasp the concept of money being sent monthly to provide for a portion of their needs. Those funds don't replace the visibility and nurturing of a parent they long to better understand.

God in His divine wisdom knew what He was doing when he ordained the institution of marriage as the ideal precursor to child bearing. It affords for balance. A balance BEST reserved for those who are fortunate to collaborate as partners in bringing children into His universe and rearing them together.

MY DADDY SHOULD HAVE TOLD ME ABOUT MALCOM X
~Amin Imamu Ojuok

I have known and mentored Amin since the age of 19.
He now mentors me. He owns his own African centered school,
The Uhuru Academy and is a spiritual leader
for the New African Temple.

My daddy should've taught me about Malcolm X. Let me tell you a story. It's a story of a young man that longed for his father but seldom got him. A young man that worked hard in school, followed the rules, and stayed out of trouble in an attempt to impress a father that didn't seem to care. It's a story of a little boy that thought his daddy didn't want him because he wasn't tough enough so he picked fights in the neighborhood. A boy that thought his daddy didn't want him because he wasn't athletic enough, so he played sports. This is a story of a little boy that loved his father anyway.

My father and I didn't have a strong relationship until maybe a year prior to his transition. Before that, though we got along great. We didn't see each other much. Growing up, my father neglected me and once I became an adult, I neglected him. I was an excellent student in school. Attending a predominantly Black high school named after an African American writer, one would think that it's students received a heavy dose of African history. Unfortunately, nothing could be further from the truth.

Graduating at the top of my class in 1990, voted Most Intellectual, named Outstanding Student of the Year, and receiving a full academic scholarship to Wiley College, you couldn't tell me at the time that civilization wasn't started by the Greeks, Adam and Eve wasn't white, and neither was God and Jesus. Black people came from white people that burned in the sun; and though slavery was bad it was better than living in Africa. Oh, and I definitely wasn't an African!

It wasn't until I got to college, and was forced to take an Intro to Black Studies course due to the fact all the other elective courses were full, that my eyes began to open. It was in this class, taught by Dr. AJ Stovall, that I began to truly understand who we are as a people and where we come from. I'd had several conversations with my father over the years, mostly superficial, and we never spoke about history or racism. As a matter of fact, I had never spoken to anyone in my family about those subjects, so exposure to this information, needless to say, had an instant and profound effect on my life.

Dr. Stovall assigned us "The Autobiography of Malcolm X" as a required read. I neglected the assignment at first, thinking it unimportant. After all, I was making an A in linear algebra, statistics, and calculus at the same time. Surely, a little Black history class wasn't going to be a problem. Lol, once Dr. Stovall let us know that not completing the readings would doom our grades resulting in the loss of my scholarship, I read the book.

Boom! That book changed my life! Reading about Malcolm, his childhood years, his years in prison, then his reformation and ascension to being one of the foremost Black leaders of all time, shifted my paradigm and awakened a thirst for knowledge inside of me that I never had before. I went on to dedicate my life to the upliftment of African people through African centered education. I currently own and operate the Uhuru Academy, Ft. Worth's only African centered school.

One of the last conversations my father and I had was about a year before he transitioned in 2003. I was going through his closet and noticed we had similar tastes in hats. We began to talk about his life and he shared some things with me that I never knew. I didn't know that he had to steal to survive as a little boy in Jefferson, Texas. I didn't know that we were descendants of enslaved Africans on the Parker Plantation in Jefferson. I didn't know he had been in the Air Force and was once a driver for Isaac Hayes.

But most importantly, my father shared with me that he was a supporter of Malcolm X! He broke down Malcolm's philosophy and told me that he related more to doing for self, which made sense because my father always owned his own business. He said that he loved what I stood for, and the work I did in the community and that he was proud of me. That was a great moment in my life, however, I couldn't help but feel a little bittersweet because my father could've told me about Malcolm X when I was a child! He could've taught me the principle of doing for self, entrepreneurship, and financial independence a long time ago! If only he had been a part of my life early on, perhaps when I made the decision to turn my back on a promising academic and subsequent professional life, I wouldn't have been as confused and in conflict with myself over taking the "road less travelled." Perhaps, I would've known why I hated working in corporate America or why I always had tense relationships with my supervisors. I had been a disciple of Malcolm all my life and didn't know it. If only my father would've told me.

HOW TO AVOID KILLING YOUR DREAMS
~Larry Kemp

Current CEO of Kemp & Sons and my fellow brother in the Alpha Phi Alpha Fraternity, Inc. I have known Larry for over 15 years. We have collaborated through his Kemp Leadership Program to impart liberating information to opportunity youth.

How can we avoid killing our dreams? The measure of personal success is not found in the challenges and/or obstacles we have to overcome but in the magnitude of one's dreams. Don't ever give in, or concede to words such as "can't, never, no, or maybe." Eliminate these kinds of words from your conversations and understanding.

Know that everyone can not and will not be with you on your journey, nor can you drag them along. The weight will be a struggle too difficult to overcome. Family members, friends and associates may not and will not be able to embrace your dream. Your dreams are for your eyes; from the depths of your internal God-given imagination. Rid yourself of the fear of failure. 99% of those who don't succeed, don't actually fail, the quit. Never give in before the manifestation of the dream, task or endeavor, persevere until you reach the dream.

Your belief has to match your work ethic. Your dream must take top priority in your life. Operate in certainty, you must see the end at the beginning.

Whatever you seek to do, don't be motivated by success or money. Success and money are simply ways to keep score, one does his best when motivated by the passion of his dreams.

"What you do speaks so loudly, I can not hear a word you say." Ralph Waldo Emerson.

WHAT MY DADDY SHOULD HAVE TOLD ME ABOUT THE KNOWLEDGE OF GOD, SELF AND OTHERS
~Student Minister Lee Muhammad

A long-time friend and spiritual partner who has supported my community work with hard-to-serve youth for over 20 years. He is the current Student Minister of Mosque 52.

My daddy should have told me to be myself regardless of what others say to me or about me, to love myself for who and what I am.

To know that my creator did not make a mistake when He brought me on the planet. There is power in being myself because no one can surpass me in being me.

Be proud of my individual uniqueness. There was none like me before and there will never be one like me again.

My daddy should have told me to read, study and research the history of my own people, the truth about slavery and to know the struggles of those who came before us and paved the way to be where we are today.

If I desire to be great, I must study greatness. Study and learn of all the great leaders who gave their lives for the freedom and liberation of their people whether they were considered controversial or not. By studying the great ones I will be able to see the realm of my own possibilities.

Throughout my education, I was taught of a few selected leaders but never the full spectrum of Black leadership. I was never taught of The Honorable Elijah Muhammad, Malcolm X (Malik El- Hajj Shabazz) or The Honorable Minister Louis Farrakhan.

My Daddy should have told me, to not rely on any teacher or school system to teach me the knowledge of my own, but to venture into a library or bookstore to learn of their views, plans, struggles and sacrifices they made, in the past and the present.

My daddy should have told me that real men pray, and real men constantly seek refuge in the Lord of The Worlds. Real men seek the help of Allah (God) because real men are always found doing something outside of their comfort zone. We only need Allah (God's) help, if we are doing something to make a difference in our world.

My daddy should have told me to always have an agenda. Know what you want to be, do and have. He should have told me that under any situation no matter how trying, to always work. Work for self, family, community and nation.

My daddy should have told me of the immeasurable value of women. That a nation can rise no higher than it's woman. Every woman should be treated with honor and respect because through her a better nation of people can and will be produced. Mother bears us in fainting and pain to bring forth life and loves us unconditionally.

A good wife stands not behind a man, but by his side to offer comfort and help in keeping our duty and reaching our goals and objectives. A daughters first love is her father and she will seek out a man like him, so we should always be mindful of her seeing the highest example of Manhood.

My daddy should have told me to seek out those spiritual guides who would serve as a guide post that would ultimately lead me to the knowledge of God and the knowledge of self. I should never worship or get stuck on the spiritual guide but to continue my journey to develop a personal relationship with my creator.

My daddy should have told me that even though I may carry his DNA and may even exhibit certain characteristics of his, that it is ok to have a spiritual father that will father you into the knowledge of God and self that you may go further then those who proceeded you.

I thank Allah (God) for the day I met such a spiritual father in the Honorable Minister Louis Farrakhan!

"A MEXICAN MAN'S THOUGHTS"
~Rubin Rayes

Ruben is a mentee of someone I mentored, Jacinto Ramos, at the time of this writing, current Fort Worth ISD School Board President. Ruben is completing his Masters degree, in pursuit of a Doctorate degree. I have known Ruben for three years working with the Youth Advocate Program.

Within the haven of my restless solitude, I often reflect, what kind of man I aspire to be?

Should one be one of those valiant, manly, brave men hardened by war in a nostalgic Mexican past or from the revolution as Pancho Villa was?

My eyes begin to water as I think of men the likes of Jose Maria Morelos and Miguel Hidalgo y Costilla, who never shrouded their sorrows with a vanishing veil and who died for their justice, land and freedom.

And more for those brave men who by the desire to practice their religion died in the wars of the Cristeros, tragically shot by an unwavering loyalty to Our Lady of Guadalupe.

Maybe I should look for the answer in my own past,

In a pernicious nostalgia, in the environment that has produced me, the root that has given life to this fruit.

It stings to remember those pitfalls I experienced during my childhood without a father.

Time passed, but a mother, who gave me life, whom I never had to ask for anything, took the role of the father in his absence.

There was no need to cultivate anything in the fields of our little minds, because we watched the brackish auroroa she dealt with every night and day.

Two jobs she had to clothe us, her small children, that through no fault of their own suffered the failures of a male parent walking a reckless path.

Two fists she had to fight those evil forces that beset us, those who would hurt us, and of extremeties in a huge world.

These words said to me,
"Take care of her, son."
My sister, who I cared for in those murky days,
days I thought would last forever.

She had two arms,
To support us in any difficulty,
To support and to embrace us on our birthdays,
To carry us when we got sick.
Two extremely strong legs she had,
To move forward and never retreat.
I know with certainty that this woman would have
sacrificed everything for her children, their blood, their
family. With her faith wrapped up in her soul, and the
primordial mission to protect us at all costs.
This woman was stronger than a man.
This woman had no cowardice,
She would never let us go hungry
Would never leave.

Would never say we were worthless,
Would never lay a hand on us.
After seeing and feeling her actions,
And after the multitude of lessons,
it was thanks to my dear mother
That I learned what it means to be a man.

WHAT MY DADDY SHOULD HAVE TOLD ME ABOUT THE VALUE OF EDUCATION
~Darron Turner

Long-time friend, golf partner, confidante and frat brother of Alpha Phi Alpha Fraternity, Inc. Darron is the Assistant Vice Chancellor, Student Affairs, Texas Christian University

I am Dr. Darron Turner the product of Jay and Ethel Turner, 3rd Ward and South Park areas of Houston, Texas. Education has always been important in my family. As the eldest son of Jay Turner, it was not without its trials.

My father didn't give a lot of hugs or accolades in my early years. He was about the business of raising his kids to be competent adults, but more so raising his sons to be men.

My dad was a strict disciplinarian. He was very serious about school. Good grades were our passport to extracurricular activities. His rules were very simple: (1) go to school, (2) pay attention and, (3) do your work. "Anything other than that, then you have done the wrong thing," he would say.

While in middle school, my father removed me from athletics for a year for making a "C" in a class. While education was important, the understanding of what it would mean later in life was not as clear. What I wish my father had talked to me about was the details of why education was pivotal to the kinds of relationships I wanted to develop, my cultural understanding and my own self-preservation.

For as long as I can remember, the idea of manhood has been bantered around at my parents' home, the community, church, school, standing on the corner or hanging out at the park playing basketball. The conversation had a life of its own in the community. Everyone had their idea of what being a man meant. The definitions were as different as the conversations we had with one another. While many views were presented, we never settled with one definition from which we could build our argument for manhood. Men and boys, young and old shared ideas about current identities and future aspirations as it related to their theory of the day.

From local ministers to the neighborhood drug dealers and all the professions in between, the conversations represented the consciousness of Black men in my neighborhood. Your ability to articulate your opinion, breakdown others' arguments gave you more time to be heard. College degrees were only beneficial if it bestowed upon the holder an expanded oratorical excellence. The paper in and of itself, provided no pivotal advantage in the street debate.

I loved the 70's and 80's era. I learned to defend my thoughts and positions on a variety of issues from the people who established standards from which many of us functioned. I enjoyed the benefits of male mentors and role models across the professional spectrum. While not all these men worked within the established rules and regulations of the community and law enforcement, they all passed along valuable life lessons. These men were critical in laying the groundwork for the man I would become.

My early years as a student athlete was spent fighting "the man" and "the system," but without the proper training or artillery. I spent more time angry because it seemed as though everyone else was getting a break, but I couldn't seem to catch one.

So I prepared to do what you do when you are losing the battle – raise the white flag, quit, leave. But God intervened and sent my next mentor who was the Chief of Police and BLACK. Like my father, he was no nonsense. We spent many days examining my behaviors as well as talking about what I wanted to accomplish.

Most importantly he reminded me that you win nothing by quitting. I was accustomed to seeing the world through the lens of my small community. If I was going to succeed, I needed to look beyond my own experiences. I'm thankful to the strong, male role models who helped me do just that.

ONE THING MY DADDY DID TELL ME
~Robert Nelson

I have known Robert Nelson for more than 20 years. We work together with youth entrepreneurship. He is a top salesman and author of "The Greatest Sales Training In the World."

"Your name is only as valuable as your word, and if your word is good your name can be priceless." My dad actually did tell me this in the best way he knew how. I was struggling with indecision in my life at the time. I was going to church and trying to lead a righteous life and on the other hand I wanted to still maintain relationships with friends that were not so receptive to my newfound change in behavior and my desire to stop old habits that were not taking me in a positive direction.

They felt like I was separating myself from them and insinuating that I was better than them in some way. I just wanted to be better and do better than I was doing and I knew that what I was doing at the time was not taking me in the direction that I wanted to go. My dad simply said to me "Son, if you make a decision for your life, stand by your decision, or don't say you are going to do something that you are not willing to back up with action!" His words have had a deep and lasting impact on my life and since then I have come to understand that his words meant far more than I was able to understand at the time.

Every time you speak any word regarding what you are willing or not willing to do, you are establishing a value. Every time you keep your word you are establishing your own value in the eyes of all whoever heard you speak that word. That value becomes associated with your identity; it is who you are or who people see you as being. That is your name. The more frequently you keep your word the more value you add to your name. If you keep your word often enough there will come a time when all you have to say is your name and your words will be accepted as gold.

That is exactly what happens when you make a promise to pay a creditor and you follow through and do it, your credit rating goes up. Conversely, if you don't keep your word your credit rating goes down and you lose all your credibility, your name holds little or no value and no matter what you say people will not believe you or accept what you're saying no matter how valuable what you are saying may be. When you learn to stand behind your word and keep it there will come a time when all you will have to do is mention your name to have whatever you desire be granted because of the priceless value you have built into your word.

In closing, I did not grow up with my father. As a matter of fact I did not meet him until my 17th birthday. I probably had a chance to see my dad about 47 times before he died. I did not get it then but I got it now. Thanks dad for teaching me that my name is only as valuable as my word.

THE CREDIT MY DADDY DESERVES
~Fredrick Darden II

I have been mentoring Fred for about 10 years. He is co-owner of his own restoration business, 911 Restoration. He is a single-parent with one son and a strong belief in God.

If I had to write one statement I wouldn't be able to give my father the credit he deserves. I love my father, I respect my father and I honor my father. He has taught me more things than any one man could ever teach his son. Even if he taught me on purpose, on accident, consciously, or unconsciously he has taught me a great deal. He has taught me to be just like him in some areas, or totally different from what he has done, to not continue that family curse in my own blood line.

One of the main things that my dad should have taught me is a mixture of what he did teach me but life had to teach me the rest of it. My dad taught me was "Work" if you want something, "GET OFF YOUR ASS AND GO GET IT, life isn't going to give you anything." The second half of life had to teach me that "You are responsible of your actions and your situation is a result of YOUR OWN decisions."

So, "you have to work for everything and you will reap the results of what you contribute and take responsibility of your actions." Own up to your responsibility and don't deflect that responsibility of the decision that you made to someone else that doesn't deserve it or isn't strong enough to handle the responsibility. Don't blame the world, don't blame your family, don't blame your spouse and don't blame your GOD when you made the decision.

You made a conscious decision to do whatever you did so take responsibility good or bad. It's okay to make mistakes, but learn from them and understand that a MAN will take full responsibility of his actions.

A POEM BY
~Devon Lacy

*A young man I've mentored from high school to Jarvis
Christian College, now attending Dallas Baptist University
working on a Masters in Communication*

Now as I endeavor I need him more than ever.
Through our souls we'll be together because nothing last
forever. La joie de vivre, but who would I be if I only
prepared you for the pleasures… not how pain will leave
you mystified when the source is unidentified. My
identity was my source and my source passed away.
Face to face with the posing question, if he were here
what would he say? In the devil's playground pay
attention to the crowd and find yourself another way.
Here idle time is the devil's time and a friend of yours is
the role he'll play. God bless the child that can find their
own remember this when feeling alone or if you realize
you're the only one don't fret, the journey to an abundant
life is a lonely one. -Jon Deaux

A GOOD BLACK MAN
Dedicated to Mothers of the African-American Male

Good Black men are indeed all around us. We pass them on the streets, in the malls and the halls at work. Most we can't see because we don't know what a good man really looks like.

He usually isn't flashy enough or rich enough to turn our heads. He might not wear a suit or push a Lexus.

He might not have a body like Tyson with a Denzel face. But, as you mature, you realize it's better to find someone who's got your back rather than someone who turns your head.

A good man doesn't agree wholeheartedly with everything you say. He doesn't just tell you what you want to hear and do the opposite. He doesn't declare how sensitive, sweet, caring, sincere, yada, yada he is. (He won't have to because it shows). He has his own opinions and yours may clash, but he doesn't have to degrade you to prove he's right. He even admits at times to being wrong, especially if you are willing to do the same. A good man is not going to meet every item on your checklist. He is human with frailties and faults mixed in with all of his wonderful, strong attributes. He needs your love and respect. HELLO!!

He needs to feel that you don't live to catch him doing something wrong so you can declare, 'Aha! I knew you were a dog!!' A good man isn't insecure about his woman having great achievements. In fact, he is her number one supporter and becomes disappointed with her when she begins to lose herself, for the sake of not hurting his feelings, or just want to make him happy.

His happiness comes with seeing her excel in her dreams and accomplishing her goals. A good man doesn't necessarily give you a huge birthday or Valentine's gift. He shows his love in the ways that are comfortable to him. Don't judge him by TV standards. No one is really living a fairy-tale. You'll miss out on your own fairy tale by buying into the myth that our men are no good. It's just not true! Black Men, we salute you, and thank you for who you are and all you've done.

Pass this along to some of the Good Black men you know and a few women that need to read it ... so that they can recognize a Good Black Man. ~Author Unknown

ABOUT THE AUTHOR

No one defies stereotypes, generalizations or clichés more than Rickie Clark. Growing up poor in Chicago, Illinois raised by a single mother on the south side, Rickie was told by a high school teacher that he was "not college material." Fortunately, there was another teacher who believed that he was destined for more.

Rickie applied to several schools and was accepted at Jarvis Christian College where he received his B.S. in Mathematics, launching a life-long career working with youth in underserved communities.

Rickie's energetic and unique approach to working with youth, particularly young men of color and those labeled "at-risk" has proven successful. In more than 20 years of community work, through his Da Village organization, Rickie has assisted more than 1,500 youth to either complete high school, obtain a GED or go on to college.

For the past 18 years he has also worked with the Everman Independent School District through his alternative community based program, Strategies to Elevate People (STEP). His passion is working with inner city, at-risk youth. He has been instrumental in helping many youth society has given up on to recognize and achieve their greater potential. He embraces the philosophy in order to be a man you must see a man.

APPENDIX A

Suggested books:

Countering the Conspiracy to Destroy Black Boys (Jawanza Kunjufu)

Vision for the Black for the Black Man (Na'im Akbar)

The Autobiography of Malcolm X (Told By Alex Haley)

Think and Grow Rich the Black Choice (Dennis Kimbro)

Empowering African-American Males to Succeed (Mychal Wynn)

Do You (Russell Simmons)

Black Man Obsolete Single and Dangerous (Haki R. Madhubuti)

APPENDIX B

Suggested Poems:

I am the Black Man (Jawanza Kunjufu)

If (Rudyard Kipling)

We Knew Not (Anthony Browder)

Just a Minute (Benjamin E Mays)

The Test of a Man (Author unknown)

If You Want Anything Bad Enough (Les Brown)

If You Think You Can (Author unknown)

APPENDIX C

Suggested Movies:

Malcolm X

James Brown

Martin Luther King

Cry Freedom- Stevin Biko

Nelson Mandala

Marcus Garvey

Hidden Colors I, II, and III

Invite Rickie Clark to Speak

Rickie goes one step beyond those proven practices to equip young men with sustainable knowledge and skills that they can retain for a life time. Rickie is a gifted communicator who offers encouragement, motivation, and inspiration to all those who come into his path. His genuine transparency comes through in the examples he gives his audiences as he guide them to manhood intentionally, consciously and purposefully. Rickie loves to provide trainings and workshops for school districts, community organization and faith based organization.

As a master facilitator, Rickie guides interactive dialog, along with providing useful and thought-provoking information for workshops, seminars, and men's retreats in the church or corporate realm.

He is also available for faith based or corporate training events and keynotes.

Rickie Speaks to:

- Youth groups
- Schools
- Church's
- Leaders
- Youth Entrepreneur's
- Corporations
- Organizations serving youth

Most Requested Presentations:

- What my Daddy Should Have Told Me, Life Lessons for the African-American Male
- Male Socialization
- Youth Entrepreneurship
- Africa the beginning of Civilization

Most Requested Trainings:

- Violence Prevention
- Rites of Passage
- Youth Entrepreneurship
- Peaceful Alternatives To Tough Situations (PATTS)

Contact Rickie at rickieclark.net or step2700@msn.com to discuss the ideal program for your next event.

31540280R00057

Made in the USA
San Bernardino, CA
12 March 2016